CONGREGATIO
OF CONSECRATEI
OF APC

D0872654

KEEP WATCH!

YEAR OF CONSECRATED LIFE

A LETTER TO CONSECRATED MEN AND WOMEN
JOURNEYING IN THE FOOTSTEPS OF GOD

Libreria Editrice Vaticana
United States Conference of Catholic Bishops
Washington, DC

Always on the road borne along by the virtue that is of pilgrims: joy!

—Pope Francis, Address, May 10, 2014

Contents

Dear Brothers and Sisters,

1. Let us continue with joy our journey toward the Year of Consecrated Life, so that our preparation may itself be a time of conversion and grace. By his words and actions, Pope Francis continues to demonstrate the fruitfulness of a life lived according to the counsels of the Gospel and the joy that lies in proclaiming this, as he invites us to go forward, to be "a Church which goes forth,"[1] according to a logic of freedom.

He urges us to leave behind us "a worldly Church with superficial spiritual and pastoral trappings," in order to breathe "the pure air of the Holy Spirit who frees us from self-centeredness cloaked in an outward religiosity bereft of God. Let us not allow ourselves to be robbed of the Gospel!"[2]

Consecrated life is a sign of good things to come in human civilization, as it travels onward "in exodus" along the paths of history. It is willing to come to grips with provisional certainties, with new situations and challenges as they develop, with the clamorous demands and passions of contemporary humanity. In this watchful pilgrimage it preserves the search for the face of God, lives in discipleship to Christ, and allows itself to be guided by the Spirit, so as to live its love for the Kingdom with creative faithfulness and ready diligence. Its

---

1   Pope Francis, Apostolic Exhortation *Evangelii Gaudium* (November 24, 2013), nos. 20-24.

2   Ibid., no. 97.

identity as a pilgrim and prayerful presence on the threshold of history (*in limine historiae*) belongs to its very nature.

This letter is intended to hand down to all consecrated men and women this valuable heritage, exhorting them "to remain faithful to the Lord in firmness of heart" (Acts 11:23) and to continue on this journey of grace. We would now like to review the steps taken over the past fifty years. In this, the Second Vatican Council emerges as an event of fundamental importance for the renewal of consecrated life. The invitation of the Lord resonates for us: "Stand by the earliest roads, ask the pathways of old, 'Which is the way to good?' and walk it; thus you will find rest for yourselves" (Jer 6:16).

In this resting-place (*statio*), each of us can recognize the seeds of life: both those that, finding a home *in a good and generous heart* (Lk 8:15), have come to fruitfulness, and those which have fallen along the wayside, on the stones or among the thorns, and have not borne fruit (see Lk 8:12-14).

We are presented with the possibility of continuing our journey with courage and watchfulness so as to make daring choices that will honor the *prophetic* character of our identity, "a special form of sharing in Christ's prophetic office, which the Holy Spirit communicates to the whole People of God,"[3] so that people today may see "the unsurpassed breadth of the strength of Christ the King and the

---

3   Pope John Paul II, Post-Synodal Apostolic Exhortation *Vita Consecrata* (March 25, 1996), no. 84.

infinite power of the Holy Spirit marvelously working in the Church."[4]

To search the horizons of our life and our times, in watchful prayer; to peer into the night in order to recognize the fire that illuminates and guides, to gaze into the heavens, looking for the heralds of blessing for our dryness. To keep awake and watch, and to make intercession, firm in faith.

The time is short to align ourselves with the Spirit who creates:

> "In our personal life, in our private lives," continued the Pope, "the same thing happens: the Spirit pushes us to take a more evangelical path, and we [say]: 'But no, it goes like this, Lord.' . . . Do not put up resistance to the Holy Spirit: this is the grace for which I wish we would all ask the Lord; docility to the Holy Spirit, to that Spirit who comes to us and makes us go forward on the path of holiness, that holiness of the Church which is so beautiful."[5]

This letter is founded in remembrance of the abundant grace experienced by consecrated men and women in the Church, and also makes a frank call for discernment. The

---

4   Second Vatican Council, *Dogmatic Constitution on the Church (Lumen Gentium)*, no. 44.

5   Pope Francis, *The Spirit Is Not Subdued*, Morning Meditation in the Chapel of the *Domus Sanctae Marthae*, Rome (April 16, 2013).

Lord is living and working in our history, and is calling us to collaboration and to collective discernment, so as to inaugurate new seasons of prophecy in the service of the Church, looking forward to the coming Kingdom.

Let us arm ourselves with the weapons of light, freedom, and the courage of the Gospel, and search the horizon, looking for the signs of God there and obeying him, making bold evangelical choices in the manner of the humble and the small.

DEPARTING OBEDIENTLY IN EXODUS

Whenever the cloud rose from the tabernacle, the Israelites would set out on their journey. But if the cloud did not lift, they would not go forward; only when it lifted did they go forward. The cloud of the LORD was over the tabernacle by day, and fire in the cloud at night, in the sight of the whole house of Israel in all the stages of their journey.

(Ex 40:36-38)

With Open Ears

2. The life of faith is not simply something we have, but a journey that has its bright stretches and dark tunnels, its open horizons and tortuous, uncertain paths. Out of God's mysterious self-abasement, coming down into our lives and our affairs, comes, according to the Scriptures, joy and amazement, gifts from God that fill life with meaning and light, and find their fullness in the messianic salvation accomplished by Christ. (Or is it the self-abasement that finds its fulfilment in Christ's messianic salvation?)

Before focusing our attention on the Second Vatican Council and its effects, let's take our cue from an iconic episode of the Bible to offer a living and grateful commemoration of the postconciliar moment of opportunity, its *kairos*, with its values that still inspire us.

The grand epic of the Exodus of the chosen people from slavery in Egypt to the Promised Land becomes an evocative icon. It suggests our modern stop and go, pause and resume, patience and enterprise. The decades since the Council have been a period of real highs and lows, of surges and disappointments, of explorations and nostalgic refusals.

The interpretative tradition of the spiritual life, which has taken various forms closely connected to the forms of consecrated life, has often found, in the great paradigm of the exodus of the people of Israel from Egypt, evocative symbols and metaphors: the burning bush, the crossing of the Red Sea, the journey through the desert, the theophany on Sinai; also the fear of the lonely wilderness, the gift of the law and of the covenant, the column of cloud and fire; manna, water from the rock, murmuring and the backsliding.

Let's take the symbol of the cloud (in Hebrew *'anan*),[6] which mysteriously guided the people on their journey: it did so by stopping, sometimes for a long time, so causing inconvenience and provoking complaint; and then rising up and moving to indicate the pace of the journey, under the guidance of God.

Let's listen to the Word:

> Whenever the cloud rose from the tabernacle, the Israelites would set out on their journey. But if the cloud did not lift, they would not go forward; only when it lifted did they go forward. The cloud of the LORD was over the tabernacle by day, and fire in the cloud at night, in the sight of the whole house of Israel in all the stages of their journey. (Ex 40:36-38)

---

6 The term *'anan* occurs eighty-seven times in the Old Testament; twenty times in Exodus and twenty more in Numbers. The expression "pillar of fire and cloud" appears only once (Ex 14:24); generally it is referred to as a "pillar of cloud" or "pillar of fire." Both expressions describe the manifestation of the divine presence.

The parallel text in Numbers (see Num 9:15-23) adds an interesting element, focusing on the stops and starts:

> Whether the cloud lingered over the tabernacle for two days or for a month or longer, the Israelites remained in camp and did not break camp; but when it lifted, they broke camp. (Num 9:22)

Clearly, this style of presence and guidance on the part of God demanded constant watchfulness: both to respond to the unpredictable movement of the cloud, and to preserve faith in God's protective presence when stops became lengthy and the final destination seemed to be indefinitely postponed.

In the symbolic language of the biblical account, the cloud was the "angel of God," as the book of Exodus affirms (Ex 14:19). In subsequent interpretation, the *cloud* becomes a privileged symbol of the presence, goodness and active faithfulness of God. In fact, the prophetic, psalmic and sapiential traditions would often revisit this symbol, developing other aspects, such as, for example, God's hiding of himself because of the fault of his people (see Lam 3:44), or the majesty of the throne of God (see 2 Chr 6:1; Jb 26:9).

The New Testament sometimes uses analogous language to revisit this symbol in the theophanies—the virginal conception of Jesus (see Lk 1:35), the transfiguration (see Mt 17:1-8), Jesus's ascension into heaven (see Acts 1:9). Paul also uses the cloud as a symbol of baptism (see 1 Cor 10:1), and the symbolism of the *cloud* is always a part of the imagery for describing the glorious return of the Lord at the end of time (see Mt 24:30; 26:64; Rev 1:7; 14:14).

To summarize, the dominant perspective, already found in the characteristic symbolism of the exodus, is that of the cloud as a sign of the divine message, the active presence of the Lord God in the midst of his people. Israel must always be ready to continue its journey if the cloud starts moving, to recognize its faults and detest them when its horizon becomes obscure, to be patient when stops are prolonged and the destination appears unreachable.

To the complexity of the multiple biblical recurrences of the symbol of the *cloud* we should add further factors: the inaccessibility of God, his sovereignty watching over all from above, his mercy that parts the clouds and comes down to bring back life and hope. Love and knowledge of God can be learned only on a journey of discipleship, in an openness free from fear and nostalgia.

Centuries after the exodus, almost on the verge of the coming of the Redeemer, the author of Wisdom would recall that adventurous epic of the Israelites led by the cloud and by the fire in an eloquent phrase: "you furnished the flaming pillar, a guide on the unknown way" (Wis 18:3).

Guided by the Cloud

3. The cloud of light and fire, which guided the people according to rhythms demanding total obedience and total watchfulness, speaks eloquently to us. We can glimpse, as in a mirror, an interpretive model for consecrated life in our time. For several decades now, consecrated life, spurred on by the charismatic impulse of the Council, has walked as if it were following the signals of the *cloud* of the Lord.

In the hearts of those who have had the grace to "see" the beginning of the conciliar journey echo the words of Pope John XXIII: *Gaudet Mater Ecclesia*, the *incipit* of the inaugural address of the Council (October 11, 1965).[7]

Under the banner of joy, the profound rejoicing of the spirit, consecrated life has been called to continue, in renewal, its journey through history:

> "In the present order of things, Divine Providence is leading us to a new order of human relations which, by men's own efforts and even beyond their very expectations, are directed toward the fulfilment of God's superior and inscrutable designs. And

---

7   Pope John XXIII, Address for the Opening of the Council *Gaudet Mater Ecclesia*, Rome (October 11, 1962).

everything, even human differences, leads to the greater good of the Church . . . perfect conformity to the authentic doctrine, which, however, should be studied and expounded through the methods of research and through the literary forms of modern thought. The substance of the ancient doctrine of the deposit oif faith is one thing, and the way in which it is presented is another. And it is the latter that must be taken into great consideration with patience if necessary."[8]

Pope John Paul II called the conciliar event "*the great grace bestowed on the Church in the twentieth century*: there we find a sure compass by which to take our bearings."[9] Pope Francis has reiterated that "was a beautiful work of the Holy Spirit."[10]

We can affirm the same thing with regard to consecrated life: the Council was a most positive experience of enlightenment and discernment, of strenuous efforts and great joys.

---

8   Ibid., "The Origin and Reason for the Second Vatican Ecumenical Council," and "Principle Duty of the Council." Translation taken from *The Documents of Vatican II*, ed. Walter M. Abbott, 712, 715.

9   Pope John Paul II, Apostolic Letter *Novo Millennio Ineunte* (January 6, 2001), no. 57.

10 Pope Francis, *The Spirit Is Not Subdued*, Morning Meditation in the Chapel of the *Domus Sanctae Marthae*, Rome (April 16, 2013). Unofficial translation of the Italian.

The consecrated have truly been on a "'exodus journey.'"[11] This has been a time of enthusiasm and audacity, of inventiveness and creative fidelity, but also of fragile certainties, of improvisations and bitter disappointments. With the benefit of hindsight, we can recognize that truly there was "fire in the cloud" (Ex 40:38), and that by "unknown" paths the Spirit in truth led the lives and plans of consecrated men and women along the paths of the Kingdom.

In recent years the impulse of this journey seems to have lost its vigor. The cloud appears to enclose more darkness than fire, but the *fire* of the Spirit still dwells in it. Although at times we may walk in darkness and a lukewarmness that threaten to trouble our hearts (see Jn 14:1), faith reawakens the certainty that inside the cloud the Lord's presence is not diminished: it is "a light of flaming fire by night" (Is 4:5), as well as being darkness.

It is always a question, in faith, of starting out on "the unknown way" (Wis 18:3), like our father Abraham, who "went out, not knowing where he was to go" (Heb 11:8). It is a journey that requires radical obedience and trust, which only faith allows us to attain, and which in faith may be renewed and strengthened.[12]

11　See Pope John Paul II, Post-Synodal Apostolic Exhortation *Vita Consecrata* (March 25, 1996), no. 40.

12　See Pope Benedict XVI, Audience, Rome (January 23, 2013).

The Exodus, in Living Memory

4. There is no doubt that, at the end of the Council, consecrated men and women welcomed the deliberations of the Council Fathers with substantial adherence and sincere fervor. It was perceived that the grace of the Holy Spirit, invoked by Pope John XXIII to obtain a *renewed Pentecost* for the Church, had been at work. The intervening time, at least a decade, had seen clear evidence that a harmony of thought, aspiration and upheavals was occurring.

The Apostolic Constitution *Provida Mater Ecclesia* of 1947 recognized that a form of consecrated life could be lived by following the evangelical counsels whilst still "in the world." This was "a revolutionary gesture in the Church."[13] This official recognition came before theological reflection set out the specific outlines of secular consecration. In a way this recognition expressed a stance that

---

13   See Pope Francis, Address to Participants in the General Assembly of the Italian Conference of Secular Institutes, Rome (May 10, 2014).

would be at the heart of the Second Vatican Council: a sympathy for the world that gives rise to a new dialogue.[14]

In 1950 this dicastery, under the auspices of Pope Pius XII, convened the first World Congress of the States of Perfection. The teachings of the pontiff opened the way for an appropriate renewal (*accommodata renovation*), an expression that the Council makes its own in the Decree *Perfectae Caritatis*. This Congress was followed by others, in various contexts and on various themes, making possible during the 1950s and at the beginning of the following decade a new theological and spiritual reflection. On this well-prepared ground, the Council scattered profusely the good seed of doctrine and a wealth of concrete guidelines that we are still living today as a precious inheritance.

We are now about fifty years away from the promulgation of the Dogmatic Constitution *Lumen Gentium* of Vatican Council II, which took place on November 21, 1964. This is a memory of the highest theological and ecclesial value: "the Church has been seen as 'a people made one with the unity of the Father, the Son and the Holy Spirit.'"[15] It recognizes the centrality of the people of God redeemed by the blood of Christ, on their journey among the nations (see Acts 20:28). Filled with the Spirit of truth and holiness, they are "sent

---

14   See Pope Paul VI, Address During the Last General Meeting of the Second Vatican Council, Rome (December 7, 1965).

15   Second Vatican Council, *Dogmatic Constitution on the Church (Lumen Gentium)*, no. 4.

forth into the whole world as the light of the world and the salt of the earth (see Mt 5:13-16)."[16]

This outlines an identity firmly founded on Christ and on his Spirit, and at the same time sets forth a Church that reaches out to all cultural, social, and anthropological situations.

> The Church is destined to extend to all regions of the earth and so enters into the history of mankind. Moving forward through trial and tribulation, the Church is strengthened by the power of God's grace, which was promised to her by the Lord, so that in the weakness of the flesh she may not waver from perfect fidelity, but remain a bride worthy of her Lord, and moved by the Holy Spirit may never cease to renew herself, until through the Cross she arrives at the light which knows no setting.[17]

Lumen Gentium dedicates the whole of its sixth chapter to religious.[18] After affirming the theological principle of the "universal vocation to holiness,"[19] the Church recognizes among the multiple ways to holiness the gift of consecrated life, received from its Lord and preserved in all eras by his

---

16   See ibid., no. 9.
17   Ibid.
18   See ibid., nos. 43-47.
19   See ibid., Chapter V.

grace.[20] The baptismal root of consecration, according to the teaching of Pope Paul VI, is manifested in joy, while he indicates the way of life lived following Christ (*sequela Christi*) as a permanent and efficacious representation of the form of existence that the Son of God embraced in his earthly life. Consecrated life, finally, operates as a sign for the People of God in the fulfilment of the common Christian vocation, and manifests the grace of the Risen Lord and the power of the Holy Spirit, who works wonders in the Church.[21]

Over the course of subsequent years, these claims have remained vigorous and effective. One change that has already borne fruit today is an increased ecclesial sense, which marks out the identity of consecrated men and women, and animates their life and work.

For the first time in the course of an ecumenical Council, consecrated life was identified as a living and fruitful part of the Church's life of communion and holiness, and not as an area in need of "decrees of reform."

The same intention guided a decree whose fiftieth anniversary we are preparing to celebrate, *Perfectae Caritatis*, promulgated on October 28, 1965. In it, the radical nature of the call resounds unmistakably: "Since the ultimate norm of the religious life is the following of Christ set forth in the Gospels, let this be held by all institutes as the highest

---

20   See ibid., no. 43.
21   See ibid., no. 44.

rule."[22] This seems like an obvious and generic affirmation, but in fact it provoked a radical purification of devotional spiritualities and identities and their re-alignment with the primacy of ecclesial and social services, firm in the reverent imitation of their founders' aims.

Nothing can come before the centrality of the radical following of Christ.

The conciliar Magisterium was also open to recognizing a variety of forms of consecrated life. For the first time at such an authoritative level, apostolic institutes received clear recognition of the principle that their apostolic action belongs to the very nature of consecrated life.[23] The lay consecrated life seems to be established and recognized as a "state for the profession of the evangelical counsels which is complete in itself."[24] The secular institutes emerge with their constitutive difference, secular consecration.[25] Groundwork is laid for the rebirth of the *Ordo Virginum* and of eremitical life, as non-communal forms of consecrated life.[26]

The evangelical counsels are presented in an innovative fashion, as an existential project undertaken with its own

---

22 Second Vatican Council, *Decree on the Adaptation and Renewal of Religious Life (Perfectae Caritatis)*, no. 2a.

23 See ibid., no. 8

24 Ibid., no. 10.

25 See ibid., no. 11.

26 Code of Canon Law, promulgated by Pope John Paul II (January 25, 1983), cann. 604 and 603.

specific means and with an especially radical way of imitating Christ.[27]

Two more themes stand out, on account of the new language in which they are presented: fraternal life in common, and formation. The first finds its biblical inspiration in the Acts of the Apostles, which for centuries has inspired the aspiration to "one heart and mind" (*cor unum et anima una*, Acts 4:32). The positive recognition of the varieties of models and styles of fraternal life constitutes today one of the most significant outcomes of the innovative inspiration of the Council. Moreover, drawing upon the shared gift of the Spirit, the Decree *Perfectae Caritatis* urges the dropping of ranks and categories so as to establish communities of a fraternal character, where all have equal rights and obligations, apart from those arising from holy orders.[28]

The value and necessity of formation is laid down as the foundation of renewal: "Adaptation and renewal depend greatly on the education of religious."[29] Because of its essential nature, this principle has functioned as an axiom: it has given rise to a determined and adventurous itinerary of experiences and discernment, in which consecrated life has invested intuition, study, research time and effort.

---

27 See Second Vatican Council, *Decree on the Adaptation and Renewal of Religious Life (Perfectae Caritatis)*, nos. 12-14.

28 See ibid., no. 15.

29 Ibid., no. 18.

Joys and Struggles on the Way

5. On the basis of the conciliar guidelines, consecrated life has undertaken a long journey. In reality, this exodus has not been directed solely to searching for horizons pointed out by the Council. Consecrated men and women are encountering and coming to grips with unprecedented social and cultural realities; they are attending to the signs of the times and of different places, to the Church's pressing invitation to implement the conciliar reforms, and the rediscovery and reinterpretation of their founding charisms, as well as rapid social and cultural change. These are novel situations, calling for new and shared discernment, whilst, at the same time, destabilizing models and styles that have been repeated over time but now are incapable of conducting dialogue, in witness to the Gospel, with new challenges and opportunities.

In the Apostolic Constitution *Humanae Salutis*, with which Pope John XXIII convened the conciliar assembly of the Second Vatican Council, we read: "Indeed, we make ours the recommendation of Jesus that one should know how to distinguish the 'signs of the times' (Mt 16:4), and we seem to see now, in the midst of so much darkness, a few indications which augur well for the fate of the Church and of humanity."[30]

The Encyclical Letter *Pacem in Terris*, addressed to all men of good will, introduced as a key theological concept the "signs of the times." Among these, Pope John XXIII recognizes: the social-economic rise of the working classes; the entrance of women into public life; the formation of independent nations,[31] the protection and promotion of the rights and duties of citizens, all aware of their dignity[32]; the conviction that solutions for conflicts must be found through negotiation, without recourse to weapons.[33] He also includes among these signs the Universal Declaration of Human Rights, approved by the United Nations.[34]

The consecrated have dwelt in and made sense of these new landscapes. They have proclaimed and borne witness to the Gospel above everything else, with their lives, offering help and solidarity of all kinds, collaborating in the most varied tasks under the banner of Christian neighborliness, as people involved in an ongoing historical process. Instead of confining themselves to lamenting over the memory of

---

30   Pope John XXIII, Apostolic Constitution *Humanae Salutis* convening the Second Vatican Council (December 25, 1961), "Reasons for Confidence." Translation taken from *The Documents of Vatican II*, ed. Walter M. Abbott, 704.

31   Pope John XXIII, Encyclical Letter, *On Peace Among All Peoples (Pacem in Terris)* (April 11, 1963), nos. 24-25.

32   See ibid., nos. 45-46.

33   See ibid., no. 67.

34   See ibid., no. 75.

past eras, they have sought to enliven the social fabric and its dynamics with the Church's living tradition, tested for centuries on the crest of history, according to the disposition (*habitus*) of faith and of Christian hope.

The task presented to consecrated life by the historical landscape at the end of the twentieth century has required boldness and courageous inventiveness. For this reason, this epoch-making journey must be evaluated as a prophetic gift, religiously motivated: many consecrated made serious efforts to live the new evangelical awareness, which obliges us to side with the poor and the least, sharing their values and anguish, often at grave personal risk.[35]

Consecrated life opens itself to renewal not because it follows self-generated initiatives, nor out of a mere desire for novelty, and much less because of a reductive focus on urgent sociological matters. Mainly, in fact, it does so out of responsible obedience to the creator Spirit, who "speaks through the prophets" (see Apostles' Creed),[36] and to the promptings of the Church's Magisterium, forcefully expressed in the great social encyclicals *Pacem*

---

35   See Pope John Paul II, Apostolic Letter to the Religious of Latin America for the Fifth Centenary of the Evangelization of the New World, *Los Caminos del Evangelio* (June, 29, 1990), nos. 19, 21; ibid., Post-Synodal Apostolic Exhortation *Vita Consecrata* (March, 25, 1996), nos. 82, 86, 89-90.

36   The first official use of the word "prophetic" on the part of the Magisterium is found in a document of the Sacred Congregation for Religious and for Secular Institutes, *Religious and Human Development* (in Latin: *Optiones Evangelicae*) (August 12, 1980), Introduction and nos. 2, 4, 24, 27, 33. In *Vita Consecrata*, in addition to the two specific paragraphs (nos. 84-85), the term is used about thirty times, roughly a hundred if analogous expressions are counted.

in Terris (1963), *Populorum Progressio* (1967), *Octogesima Adveniens* (1971), *Laborem Exercens* (1981), and *Caritas in Veritate* (2009). This has been a question—to return to the image of the cloud—of fidelity to God's will, as manifested through the authoritative voice of the Church.

This vision of the charism of consecrated life —as something originated by the Spirit, oriented to conformation to Christ, marked by a community-based ecclesial profile, and in dynamic development within the Church—has grounded every decision of renewal; gradually, it has given rise to a true theology of the charism, applied in a clear way to consecrated life for the first time.[37] The Council did not explicitly apply this term, "charism," to consecrated life, but it opened the way for this by making reference to some of the statements of Paul.[38]

In the Apostolic Exhortation *Evangelica Testificatio*, Pope Paul VI officially adopts this new terminology[39] and writes:

> The Council rightly insists on the obligation of religious to be faithful to the spirit of their founders, to their evangelical intentions and to the example of

---

37 See Sacred Congregation for Religious and for Secular Institutes—Sacred Congregation for Bishops, *Directives for the Mutual Relations Between Bishops and Religious in the Church (Mutuae Relationes)* (May 14, 1978), nos. 12, 19, 51.

38 Cf., for example, Second Vatican Council, *Decree on the Adaptation and Renewal of Religious Life (Perfectae Caritatis)*, nos. 1, 2, 7, 8, 14, 15; *Decree on the Missionary Activity of the Church (Ad Gentes)*, no. 23

39 Pope Paul VI, Apostolic Exhortation *Evangelica Testificatio* (June 29, 1971), nos. 11, 12, 32.

their sanctity. In this it finds one of the principles for the present renewal and one of the most secure criteria for judging what each institute should undertake.[40]

This Congregation, a witness to this journey, has accompanied the different phases of rewriting of the Constitutions of the various institutes. It has been a process that has altered long-standing equilibriums and changed obsolete traditional practices,[41] while it has reinterpreted the spiritual patrimony with a new hermeneutic, and has tested new structures, to the point of reshaping programs and presences. In this renewal, faithful and creative at the same time, we should not conceal certain dialectics of confrontation, tension, and, even, painful defection.

The Church has not stopped this process, but has accompanied it with careful teaching and wise vigilance, identifying seven main themes concerning the primacy of the spiritual life: the foundational charism, life in the Spirit nourished by the Word (*lectio divina*), fraternal life in common, initial and continuing formation, new forms of apostolate, the exercise of authority and attention to different cultures. Consecrated life over the last fifty years has been measured and shaped according to these requirements.

---

40 Pope Paul VI, Apostolic Exhortation *Evangelica Testificatio* (June 29, 1971), no. 11.

41 See Second Vatican Council, *Decree on the Adaptation and Renewal of Religious Life (Perfectae Caritatis)*, no. 3.

Reference to the letter of the Council allows us to "draw from them its authentic spirit," and avoid mistaken interpretations.[42] We are called to commemorate together a living event in which we, the Church, have recognized our most profound identity. At the closing of the Second Vatican Council, with a grateful mind and heart Pope Paul VI affirmed:

> The Church has gathered herself together in deep spiritual awareness . . . to find in herself, active and alive, the Holy Spirit, the word of Christ; and to probe more deeply still the mystery, the plan and the presence of God above and within herself; to revitalize in herself that faith which is the secret of her confidence and of her wisdom, and that love which impels her to sing without ceasing the praises of God. *Cantare amantis est* (song is the expression of a lover), says St. Augustine (*Serm.* 336; PL 38, 1472).

The council documents—especially the ones on divine revelation, the liturgy, the Church, priests, religious, and the laity—leave wide open to view this primary and focal religious intention, and show how clear and fresh and rich is the spiritual stream which contact with the living God

---

42   See Pope Benedict XVI, Homily, Holy Mass for the Opening of the Year of Faith, Rome (October 11, 2012).

causes to well up in the heart of the Church, and flow out from it over the dry wastes of our world.[43]

The same loyalty toward the Council as an ecclesial event and as a model of behavior now requires that we turn with trust to the future. Is the certainty alive in us that God always guides our journey?

In its wealth of words and actions, the Church leads us to interpret our personal and community life in the context of the whole plan of salvation, to understand which direction to take, what future to imagine that is in continuity with the steps taken previous to our own day, and invites us to a rediscovery of the unity of the witness of praise, faith and life (*confessio laudis, fidei et vitae*).

The "memory of faith" (*memoria fidei*) gives us roots of continuity and perseverance: this is a powerful identity allowing us to see ourselves as part of a tale, a history. Letting faith reinterpret in the journey that has been made is not limited to the big events, but also helps us reinterpret our personal history, helpfully dividing it into episodes.

---

43   Pope Paul VI, Address During the Last General Meeting of the Second Vatican Council, Rome (December 7, 1965).

STAY AWAKE
AND
KEEP WATCH

Elijah went up to the top of Carmel, crouched down to the earth, and put his head between his knees. He said to his servant, "Go up and look out to sea."

(1 Kgs 18:42-43)

With Open Ears

6. Let's look for more light in the biblical symbolism, asking for inspiration for the journey of prophecy and of exploring new horizons of consecrated life, which we would now like to consider in this second part. Consecrated life, by its very nature in fact, is intrinsically called to serve as a witness, presenting a sign of the Church (*signum in Ecclesia*).[44]

This is a function that belongs to every Christian, but in consecrated life it is characterized by the radical nature of Christian discipleship (the *sequela Christi*) and the primacy of God, and at the same time by its capacity to live the evangelizing mission of the Church with truthfulness (*parrhesia*) and creativity. Pope John Paul II rightly reiterated that "The prophetic character of the consecrated life . . . is also expressed through the denunciation of all that is contrary to the divine will and through the exploration of new ways to apply the Gospel in history, in expectation of the coming of God's Kingdom."[45]

---

44 Second Vatican Council, *Dogmatic Constitution on the Church (Lumen Gentium)*, no. 44.

45 Pope John Paul II, Post-Synodal Apostolic Exhortation *Vita Consecrata* (March 25, 1996), no. 84.

In the patristic tradition, the biblical model of reference for monastic life is the prophet Elijah, because of his life of solitude and asceticism, his passion for the covenant and fidelity to the law of the Lord, and his audacity in defending the rights of the poor (see 1 Kgs 17-19; 21). This was also recalled by the Apostolic Exhortation *Vita Consecrata*, in support of the prophetic nature and function of consecrated life.[46] In the monastic tradition, the mantle that Elijah symbolically let fall upon Elisha at the moment of his ascent into heaven (see 2 Kgs 2:13) is interpreted as the passage of the prophetic spirit from father to disciple and also as a symbol of consecrated life in the Church, which, always new, lives by memory and prophecy.

Elijah the Tishbite suddenly appears in the narrative of the northern kingdom, with a peremptory admonition: "Elijah the Tishbite, from Tishbe in Gilead, said to Ahab: 'As the LORD, the God of Israel, lives, whom I serve, during these years there shall be no dew or rain except at my word'" (1 Kgs 17:1). He stands for a rebellion of religious conscience in the face of moral decadence, into which the people are led by the insolence of Queen Jezebel and the indolence of King Ahab. The prophetic sentence that shuts heaven is an open challenge to the special function of *Baal* and the *baalîm*, who were reckoned to control fecundity and fertility, rain and abundance. From here begins the sweeping narrative of Elijah's actions in episodes that, rather than

---

46   Ibid.

telling a story, present dramatic moments of great inspirational power (see 1 Kgs 17-19, 21; 2 Kgs 1-2).

In every event Elijah lives out his prophetic service, undergoing the purifications and enlightenments that characterize his biblical profile, until the culminating moment of his encounter with God in the soft and silent breeze on Mount Horeb. These experiences are also inspirational for consecrated life. This too must pass from the solitary and penitential refuge in the *wadi* of Cherith (see 1 Kgs 17:2-7) to the encounter with the poor fighting for their lives, like the widow of Zarephath (see 1 Kgs 17:8-24); must learn from the brilliant audacity represented by the challenge of the sacrifice on Carmel (see 1 Kgs 18:20-39) and by the intercession for the people devastated by drought and the culture of death (see 1 Kgs 18:41-46). It must defend the rights of the poor, trodden down by the high and mighty (see 1 Kgs 21), and warn against those forms of idolatry that profane the holy name of the God (see 2 Kgs 1).

One particularly dramatic episode is Elijah's deadly depression in the desert of Beersheba (1 Kgs 19:1-8); but there God, offering him the bread and water of life, is able to turn his flight into a pilgrimage to Mount Horeb (1 Kgs 19:9).

This is an example for our dark nights, which, as for Elijah, precede the splendor of the theophany in the gentle breeze (1 Kgs 19:9-18) and prepare the way for new seasons of fidelity, which become stories of new callings (as for Elisha: 1 Kgs 19:19-21), but also bring boldness to intervene against the perversion of justice (see the murder of Naboth:

1 Kgs 21:17-29). Finally, we are moved by his affectionate farewell to the communities of the children of the prophets (2 Kgs 2:1-7), in preparation for the final crossing of the Jordan, up to heaven in the fiery chariot (2 Kgs 2:8-13).

We might feel drawn to the spectacular actions of Elijah, to his furious protests, his direct and bold accusations, to his encounter with God on Horeb, when Elijah goes so far as to accuse the people of planning nothing but destruction and ruin. But let's consider that at this historic moment, there are some lesser elements that have more to say to us, which are like little signs to inspire our steps and choices in a new way in this modern age in which the footsteps of God seem to vanish, as religious sensibility becomes a desert.[47]

The biblical texts offers numerous "lesser" symbols. We can highlight: the *scarce resources* for life at the brook Cherith, and the *ravens* that obey God in bringing the prophet bread and meat, in a gesture of mercy and solidarity. The *generosity*, at the risk of her own life, of the widow of Zarephath who has only "a handful of flour" and "a little oil" (1 Kgs 17:12) and gives them to the famished prophet. The *powerlessness* of Elijah in the face of the dead boy, and his cry of doubt together with his desperate embrace, which the widow interprets in a theological way, as the revelation of the face of a compassionate God. The long struggle of the prophet, prostrate in intercession—after the spectacular and rather theatrical clash with the priests of Baal

---

47   See Pope Francis, Apostolic Exhortation *Evangelii Gaudium* (November 24, 2013), no. 86.

on Carmel—imploring rain for the people, exhausted by the sentence of drought. It is a team effort by Elijah, the boy who goes up and down from the crest, and God who, rather than Baal, is the true lord of the rain; and the answer finally comes in a *little cloud*, the size of a man's hand (see 1 Kgs 18:44). A tiny answer from God, which nonetheless quickly becomes a great rainfall, restoring a people on the brink of exhaustion.

Another outwardly poor yet effective response comes a few days later with the *loaf* and the *jar* of water that appear beside the prophet in his deathly depression in the desert: this is a resource that gives him the strength to walk "forty days and forty nights to the mountain of God, Horeb" (1 Kgs 19:8). And there, in the cleft of a cave where Elijah takes shelter, still bristling with anger against the destructive and sacrilegious people threatening even his own life, he witnesses the destruction of his conceptions of threat and power: "The Lord was not . . ." in the impetuous wind, in the earthquake, in the fire, but in "a light silent sound" (1 Kgs 19:12).[48]

This is both a sublime page for mystical literature, and a sheer drop into reality for all of the prophet's "holy rage" he has to recognize the presence of God outside all traditional

---

48 In Hebrew, *qôl demamáh daqqáh*; the translation is not easy or straightforward, because each word has several meanings. *Qôl* means voice, sound, wind, rustling, murmur, breeze, whisper; *demamáh* means silence, void of death, suspension, breathlessness; *daqqáh* means light, faint, fine, subtle, tranquil. The Septuagint translates this into Greek as *phonè aúras leptês*, Jerome into Latin as *sibilus aurae tenuis*.

conceptions, which tried to keep him prisoner. God is whisper and breeze, not a product of our need for security and success, he leaves *no visible trace of his passing* (see Ps 77:20), but is present in a true and efficacious manner.

In his fury and emotion, Elijah was about to ruin everything, deceiving himself that he alone had remained faithful. God, meanwhile, knew well that there were seven thousand faithful witnesses, and prophets and kings ready to obey him (1 Kgs 19:15-19), because God's story was not limited to the failure of a depressed and surly prophet. The story continues, because it is in the hands of God, and Elijah must look at reality with new eyes, allowing himself to be reborn in hope and trust by God himself. His crouching posture on the mountain when he is begging for rain, which so strongly resembles the unborn child in its mother's womb, is also revisited symbolically on Horeb when he takes refuge in the cave. Now it is now completed with the prophet's new birth to walk upright and regenerated on the mysterious paths of the living God.

At the foot of the mountain, the people were still fighting against a life that was no longer life, against a religiosity that was a profanation of the covenant and a new idolatry. The prophet must take upon himself that fight and that desperation, he must retrace his steps (1 Kgs 19:15), which now are God's alone, and recross the desert. The desert, however, now blossoms with new meaning, so that life may triumph and new prophets and leaders may faithfully serve the covenant.

The Prophecy of Life in Keeping with the Gospel

7. The time of grace that we are living through, with Pope Francis's insistence on placing the Gospel and what is essentially Christian at the center of things, is for consecrated men and women a new call to watchfulness, to be ready for the signs of God.[49] "There shall be no dew or rain except at my word" (1 Kgs 17:1). We have to fight against eyes weighed down with sleep (see Lk 9:32), so as not to lose the attitude of discerning the *movements of the cloud* that guides our journey (see Num 9:17) and to recognize in the *small and frail signs* the presence of the Lord of life and hope.

The Council has given us a method: the method of reflecting on the world and human events, on the Church and Christian existence, beginning with the Word of God, God who reveals himself and is present in history. This method is supported by an attitude: one of listening, that opens itself to dialogue and enriches the journey toward the truth. Returning to the *centrality of Christ and of the Word*

---

49   See Pope Francis, Apostolic Exhortation *Evangelii Gaudium* (November 24, 2013), no. 84.

of God, as the Council[50] and the subsequent Magisterium have insistently invited us to do[51] in a biblically and theologically grounded way, can be a guarantee of authenticity and quality for the future of our lives as consecrated men and women.

This is a listening that transforms us and makes us proclaimers and witnesses of the intentions of God in history and of his efficacious activity for salvation. Amidst today's needs, let's return to the Gospel, quench our thirst with the Sacred Scriptures, in which we find the "pure and everlasting source of spiritual life."[52] In fact, as Pope John Paul II aptly put it: "There is no doubt that this primacy of holiness and prayer is inconceivable without a renewed *listening to the word of God*."[53]

---

50 See Second Vatican Council, *Decree on the Adaptation and Renewal of Religious Life (Perfectae Caritatis)*, no. 5; ibid., *Dogmatic Constitution on Divine Revelation (Dei Verbum)*, nos. 21, 25.

51 See Pope John Paul II, Post-Synodal Apostolic Exhortation *Vita Consecrata* (March 25, 1996), no. 84; Pope John Paul II, Apostolic Letter *Novo Millennio Ineunte* (January 6, 2001), II. "A face to contemplate" (nos. 16-28); III. "Starting afresh from Christ" (nos. 29-41); Pope Benedict XVI, Encyclical Letter *Deus Caritas Est* (December 25, 2005); Congregation for the Institutes of Consecrated Life and Societies of Apostolic Life, Instruction *Starting Afresh From Christ: A Renewed Commitment to Consecrated Life in the Third Millennium* (May 19, 2002).

52 See Second Vatican Council, *Dogmatic Constitution on Divine Revelation (Dei Verbum)*, no. 21.

53 Pope John Paul II, Apostolic Letter *Novo Millennio Ineunte* (January 6, 2001), no. 39.

The Gospel, the Supreme Rule

8. One of the characteristics of the conciliar renewal for consecrated life has been the radical return to following Christ (the *sequela Christi*):

> Indeed from the very beginning of the Church men and women have set about following Christ with greater freedom and imitating Him more closely through the practice of the evangelical counsels, each in his own way leading a life dedicated to God.[54]

Following Christ, as proposed in the Gospel, is the "ultimate norm of the religious life" and the "highest rule"[55] of all the institutes. One of the earliest names for monastic life is "evangelical life."

The different forms of consecrated life bear witness to this evangelical inspiration, starting with Anthony, the pioneer of solitary life in the desert. His story begins with listening to the word of Christ: "If you wish to be perfect, go, sell what you have and give to [the] poor, and you will have treasure in heaven. Then come, follow me" (Mt 19:21).

From Anthony on, the monastic tradition makes Scripture its rule of life: the first Rules are simple practical norms, without any pretense of spiritual content; because

---

54   Second Vatican Council, *Decree on the Adaptation and Renewal of Religious Life (Perfectae Caritatis)*, no. 1.
55   Ibid., no. 2.

the only rule of the monk is Scripture, no other rule is admissible: "We take care to read and learn the Scriptures," writes Orsiesius, a disciple and successor of Pachomius, "and to consecrate ourselves incessantly to meditating on them . . . The Scriptures guide us to eternal life."[56]

Basil, the great master of Eastern monasticism, when he wrote the *Asceticon*,[57] destined to become the manual of monastic life, refuses to call it a *Rule*. His point of reference is instead the *Moralia*,[58] a collection of biblical texts commented on and applied to situations of life in community (*santa koinonia*). In the Basilian system, the behavior of the monks is defined through the Word of God, the God, always present, who examines hearts and minds (see Rev 2:23). This constant presence before the Lord, *memoria Dei*, is perhaps the most specific element of Basilian spirituality.

In the West, the journey moves in the same direction. The rule of Benedict is obedience to the Word of God: "Let us listen to the voice of God that speaks to us every day . . ."[59] *Listen, my son*[60]: this is the opening of the *Regula Benedicti*, because it is in listening that we become sons and disciples, in welcoming the Word that we ourselves become word.

---

56 See *Pacomio e i Suoi Discepoli .Regole e Scritti*, L. Cremaschi (ed.), Magnano 1988, p. 409.
57 Basil, *Moralia* (PG, 31, 692-869); Ibid., *Regulae fusius tractatae* (PG, 31, 889-1052).
58 Ibid., *In Regulas Brevius Tractatae* (PG, 31, 1052-1305).
59 Benedict, *Rule*, Prologue, 9.
60 Benedict, *Rule*, Prologue, 1.

In the twelfth century, Stephen of Muret, founder of the Order of Grandmont, concisely expressed this condition of being rooted in the Gospel: "If someone asks you of what profession or what rule or what order you are, respond that you are of the first and principal rule of the Christian religion, meaning the Gospel, the wellspring and principle of all rules; there is no other rule than the Gospel."[61]

The emergence of the Mendicant Orders makes, if possible, the movement of return to the Gospel even more incisive.

Dominic "showed himself everywhere to be an evangelical man, in words as in works"[62]: he was a living Gospel, capable of proclaiming what he lived, and who wanted his preachers to be "evangelical men" as well.[63]

For Francis of Assisi, the Rule is "the life of the Gospel of Jesus Christ"[64]; for Clare of Assisi: "the form of life of the order of four sisters . . . is this: 'To observe the holy Gospel of our Lord Jesus Christ.'"[65] In the rule of the Carmelites,

---

61   *Monastic Rules of the West*, Magnano 1989, pp. 216-217.

62   *Libellus* 104, in P. Lippini, *San Domenico visto da i suoi contemporanei*, Edizioni Studio Domenicano, Bologna 1982, p. 110.

63   *First Constitutions* or *"Consuetudines,"* 31. Because of this "often, both by voice and by letter, he admonished and exhorted the friars of the Order to study the Old and New Testament continually . . . He also carried the Gospel of Matthew and the epistles of Paul with him and studied them so much that he almost knew them by memory" (Deposition of Fra Giovanni di Spagna, in Domenico di Gusmán. *Il Carisma della Predicazione*, Introduction by P. Lippini, EDB, Padova 1993, p. 143).

64   *Regola non bollata, Titolo*: FF 2,2. The *Regola bollata* begins with the same tone: "The Rule and life of the friars minor is this, to observe the Holy Gospel of our Lord Jesus Christ . . ." (1, 2: FF 75).

65   *Rule* I, 1-2: FF 2750.

the fundamental precept is that of "meditating on the Law of the Lord day and night," in order to translate it into concrete action: "all that you must do, do it in the word of the Lord."[66] This foundation, common to so many religious families, remained unchanged with the passing of centuries.

In our own time, James Alberione affirmed that the Pauline Family "aspires to live the Gospel of Jesus Christ to the full,"[67] while Little Sister Magdeleine has said: "We must build something new. Something new that is old, that is the authentic Christianity of the first disciples of Jesus. We have to take up the Gospel word for word."[68] Every charism of consecrated life is rooted in the Gospel. Passion for the biblical Word is evident and significant in many of the new communities that today are flourishing all over the Church.

Today, returning to the Gospel sounds to us like a "provocation"; it takes us back to the source of every life rooted in Christ, and is a powerful invitation to undertake a journey back to the origin, to the place where our life takes shape, where every rule and norm finds meaning and value.

The Holy Father has often urged us to trust in and entrust ourselves to this life-giving dynamic: "I invite you

---

66 *Rule of Carmel*, cc. 10 and 19; see B. Secondin, *Una fraternità orante e profetica in un mondo che cambia. Rileggere la Regola del Carmelo oggi*, Perugia 2007, pp. 8 e 11.

67 G. Alberione, *"Abundantes divitiae gratiae suae." Storia carismatica della Famiglia Paolina*, Rome 1977, n. 93.

68 Piccola Sorella Magdeleine, *Il padrone dell'impossibile*, Casale Monferrato 1994, p. 201.

never to doubt the power of the Gospel, nor its capacity to convert hearts to Christ Resurrected, and to lead people on the path to salvation, which they are waiting for deep within them."[69]

Formation: Gospel and Culture

9. Formation according to the Gospel and its demands is an imperative. In this context, we have been asked to undertake a specific revision of the model of formation that accompanies consecrated men and in particular consecrated women on the journey of life. Spiritual formation is a pressing need, although very often it is limited almost entirely to simple psychological companionship or to standardized exercises of piety.

Impoverished, repetitive and vague in its content, this formation can trap the candidates in infantile and dependent levels of human growth. The rich variety of ways followed and suggested by spiritual authors remains almost unknown to direct reading, or is recalled only in fragments. It is essential to ensure the patrimony of institutes is not reduced to cursory outlines, detached from their life-giving original content, because this is not an adequate introduction to the Christian experience or to the experience of the charism.

---

69 Pope Francis, Address to the Bishops of the Episcopal Conference of Madagascar on Their *Ad Limina* Visit, Rome (March 28, 2014).

In a world in which secularization has become selective blindness toward the supernatural and men have lost sight of the footsteps of God,[70] we are called to rediscover and study the fundamental truths of the faith.[71] Those who render the service of authority are called to foster in all consecrated men and women a well-founded and consistent understanding of the Christian faith, supported by a new love of study. Pope John Paul II exhorted: "within the consecrated life itself there is a need for a *renewed and loving commitment to the intellectual life*, for dedication to study."[72] It is a reason for profound regret that this imperative has not always been accepted and far less received as a demand of radical reform for consecrated men, and in particular for consecrated women.

The weakness and fragility in this area require us to recall, and forcibly to reiterate the necessity of continual formation for an authentic life in the Spirit, and in order to remain mentally open and consistent in the journey of

---

70   See Pope John Paul II, Post-Synodal Apostolic Exhortation *Vita Consecrata* (March 25, 1996), no. 85.

71   It could also be helpful here to read and assimilate the *Catechism of the Catholic Church*, which presents a systematic and organic synthesis, in which the richness of the teaching that the Church has received, guarded and offered, emerges. "From Sacred Scripture to the Fathers of the Church, from theological masters to the saints across the centuries, the *Catechism* provides a permanent record of the many ways in which the Church has meditated on the faith and made progress in doctrine so as to offer certitude to believers in their lives of faith." Pope Benedict XVI, Apostolic Letter in the form *motu proprio, Porta Fidei*, with which he proclaimed the Year of Faith (October 11, 2011), no. 11.

72   Pope John Paul II, Post-Synodal Apostolic Exhortation *Vita Consecrata* (March 25, 1996), no. 98.

growth and fidelity.[73] There is certainly no lack of formal acceptance of this urgent need, on a theoretical level, and there is an overwhelming consensus in scholarly research on this topic, but, if we are honest, the resulting practice is fragile, scarce, and often inconsistent, confused, and noncommittal.

A witness to the Gospel is one who has encountered Jesus Christ, who knows him, or better, *who feels known by Him*, recognized, respected, loved, forgiven, and this encounter has deeply touched him, filled him with a new joy, given life a new meaning. And this shines through, it's passed on to others.[74]

The Word, the genuine source of spirituality[75] from which to draw "the supreme good of knowing Christ Jesus" (Phil 3:8), must inhabit our everyday lives. It is only in this way that its *power* (see 1 Thes 1:5) can make inroads into human frailty, can grow and build places of community life, and correct our thoughts, affections, decisions and the dialogues woven in a spirit of brotherhood. Following the example of Mary, listening to the Word must become the

---

73 See ibid., no. 71.
74 Pope Francis, Address to Members of the Apostolic Movement of the Blind (MAC) and to the Little Mission for the Deaf and Mute, Rome (March 29, 2014).
75 See Second Vatican Council, *Dogmatic Constitution on Divine Revelation (Dei Verbum)*, no. 25; Pope John Paul II, Post-Synodal Apostolic Exhortation *Vita Consecrata* (March 25, 1996), no. 94; Pope Benedict XVI, Post-Synodal Apostolic Exhortation *Verbum Domini* (September 30, 2010), no. 86.

breath of life in every moment of existence.[76] In this way our life will come together in a unity of thought, be revived in inspiration for constant renewal, and bear fruit in apostolic creativity.[77]

The Apostle Paul asked the disciple Timothy to *seek the faith* (see 2 Tm 2:22) with the same constancy as he had showed when he was a young man (see 2 Tm 3:15); in the first place, this consists in remaining firm in what he had learned, meaning the holy Scriptures: "All scripture is inspired by God and is useful for teaching, for refutation, for correction, and for training in righteousness, so that one who belongs to God may be competent, equipped for every good work" (2 Tm 3:16-17).

We should take this as an invitation addressed to us, so that no one may become lazy in the faith (see Heb 6:12). It is a life-giving companion allowing us to perceive with eyes that are always new the wonders that God works for us, and to dispose ourselves for an obedient and responsible answer.[78]

The Gospel, the true norm for the Church and for consecrated life, must represent its normative character in the Church's practice, its style and its way of being. And this

---

76   See Pope Benedict XVI, Post-Synodal Apostolic Exhortation *Verbum Domini* (September 30, 2010), no. 27.

77   Congregation for Institutes of Consecrated Life and Societies of Apostolic Life, Instruction *Starting Afresh from Christ: A Renewed Commitment to Consecrated Life in the Third Millennium* (May 19, 2002).

78   See Pope Benedict XVI, Apostolic Letter in the form *motu proprio*, *Porta Fidei*, with which he proclaimed the Year of Faith (October 11, 2011), no. 15.

is the challenge that Pope Francis has reissued. Calling for an ecclesiological rebalancing between the Church as hierarchical body and the Church as Body of Christ, he offers us materials for carrying out this operation, which can take place only in the living body (*in corpore vivo*) of the Church, meaning inside of us and through us. Evangelizing does not mean bringing a message that is recognized as being useful for the world, nor a presence that asserts itself, nor something that offends by its visibility, nor a blinding splendor; but, instead, it means proclaiming Jesus Christ, the hope within us (see Col 1:27-28), a proclamation made up of words of grace (Lk 4:22), with good conduct among men (1 Pt 2:12) and with faith that works by means of love (Gal 5:6).

The Prophecy of Watchfulness

10. At the conclusion of the conciliar assembly, Pope Paul VI—with the vision of a prophet—said farewell to the bishops gathered in Rome, uniting past tradition and future:

> In this universal assembly, in this privileged point of time and space, there converge together the past, the present and the future—the past: for here, gathered in this spot, we have the Church of Christ with her tradition, her history, her councils, her doctors, her saints; the present: for we are taking leave of one another to go out toward the world of today with its miseries, its sufferings, its sins, but also with its prodigious accomplishment, its values, its virtues; and lastly the future is here in the urgent appeal of the peoples of the world for more justice, in their will for peace, in their conscious or unconscious thirst for a higher life, that life precisely which the Church of Christ can and wishes to give them."[79]

---

79 Pope Paul VI, Address to the Council Fathers on the Occasion of the Closing of the Second Vatican Council, Rome (December 8, 1965).

Pope Francis passionately encourages us to continue on our journey, with rapid and joyful steps: "led by the Spirit, never unyielding, never closed, always open to the voice of God that speaks, that opens, that leads us and invites us to go toward the horizon."[80]

What countries do we live in, and what horizons are given to us to search?

Pope Francis calls us to welcome today, which is God's, and his "*new things*"; he invites us to welcome "God's surprises"[81] faithfully, without fear or resistance, in order to "be prophets in particular, by demonstrating how Jesus lived on this earth, and to proclaim how the kingdom of God will be in its perfection. A religious must never give up prophesy."[82]

What resounds for us is the invitation to proceed on the journey while carrying in our hearts the expectations of the world. We notice that these are both light and heavy, while we look for the unpredictable arrival of the *little cloud*. This is the humble seed of an *announcement* that cannot be silenced.

---

80 Pope Francis, Homily for the Feast of the Presentation of the Lord on the Eighteenth World Day of Consecrated Life, Rome (February 2, 2014).

81 Pope Francis, Homily for the Easter Vigil, Rome (March 30, 2013): "We are afraid of God's surprises! He always surprises us! The Lord is like that. Dear brothers and sisters, let us not be closed to the newness that God wants to bring into our lives!"

82 A. Spadaro, "Svegliate il mondo!" Conversation of Pope Francis with Superiors General, in *La Civiltà Cattolica*, 165 (2014/I), 7, quoting Spadaro's 2013 interview with Pope Francis. English translation of Spadaro's 2013 interview with Pope Francis published as "A Big Heart Open to God," *America Magazine*, September 30, 2013.

Consecrated life is living through a time of demanding transitions and new requirements. This crisis is a moment in which we are called to the evangelical exercise of discernment; it is the opportunity to choose with wisdom—like the scribe, *who draws forth from his storehouse things that are old and things that are new* (see Mt 13:52)—whilst remembering that history is tempted to preserve more things than can ever be used. We risk preserving sacralized "memories" that make it harder for us to come out of the *cave* of our comfort-zone. The Lord loves us *with everlasting affection* (see Is 54:8): this confidence calls us to freedom.

Together, we search the horizon

11. A disguised accidie (ἀκηδία) sometimes weakens our spirit, obscures our vision, enervates our decisions and numbs our steps, binding the identity of consecrated life to an old and self-referential model, to a narrow horizon: "A tomb psychology thus develops and slowly transforms Christians into mummies in a museum."[83] Against this inertia of spirit and action, against this discouragement that saddens and extinguishes soul and will, Pope Benedict XVI had already exhorted us:

> Do not join the ranks of the prophets of doom who proclaim the end or meaninglessness of the consecrated

---

83   Pope Francis, Apostolic Exhortation *Evangelii Gaudium* (November 24, 2013), no. 83.

life in the Church in our day; rather, clothe yourselves in Jesus Christ and put on the armor of light—as St. Paul urged (see Rom 13:11-14)—keeping awake and watchful. St. Chromatius of Aquileia wrote: "Distance this peril from us so that we are never overcome by the heavy slumber of infidelity. Rather may he grant us his grace and his mercy, that we may watch, ever faithful to him. In fact our fidelity can watch in Christ (*Sermon* 32, 4).[84]

Consecrated life is at a crossroads, but it cannot stay there forever. We are invited to make the transition—*an outgoing Church*, in one of the characteristic expressions of Pope Francis—into an opportune moment (*kairós*) demanding renunciation, asking us to leave behind what we know and undertake a long and difficult journey, like Abraham travelling to the land of Canaan (see Gen 12:1-6), or Moses toward a mysterious land linked to the patriarchs (see Ex 3:7-8), or Elijah to Zarephath of Sidon: each of them going to mysterious lands glimpsed only in faith.

This is not a matter of answering the question of whether what we are doing is good: discernment looks to the horizons that the Spirit suggests to the Church. It interprets the rustling of the morning stars, without looking for emergency exits or improvised shortcuts, and allows itself to be led on to great things by means of small and frail signs, and

---

84 Pope Benedict XVI, Homily for the Feast of the Presentation of the Lord on the Eighteenth World Day of Consecrated Life, Rome (February 2, 2013).

puts its meagre resources into play. We are called to a shared obedience that trusts in today, so as to travel together with "the courage to cast the nets on the *strength of his word* (see Lk 5:5) and not only from solely human motivations."[85]

Consecrated life, nourished by the hope of the promise, is called to continue its journey without allowing itself to be influenced by what it leaves behind: "I have the strength for everything through him who empowers me. Still, it was kind of you to share in my distress" (Phil 4:13-14). Hope is not built on the foundation of our strength or our numbers, but on the gifts of the Spirit: faith, communion, mission. The consecrated are people made free by the profession of the counsels of the Gospel who are willing to look in faith beyond the present, and are invited to "broaden our horizons and see the greater good which will benefit us all."[86]

The goal of this journey is marked out by the rhythm of the Spirit; it is not a known land. In front of us appear new frontiers, new realities, other cultures, different necessities, *peripheries.*

In imitation of the teamwork of the prophet Elijah and his servant, we must recollect ourselves in prayer with a sense of passion and compassion for the good of the people who live in situations of disorientation and often of pain. Also critical is the generous and patient service of

85 Congregation for Institutes of Consecrated Life and Societies of Apostolic Life, Instruction *The Service of Authority and Obedience*. *Faciem tuam, Domine, Requiram* (May 11, 2008), no. 11.
86 Pope Francis, Apostolic Exhortation *Evangelii Gaudium* (November 24, 2013), no. 235.

the servant, who climbs again to look out to sea, until he glimpses the little *signal* of a new story, of a "heavy rain" (1 Kgs 18:45). That *gentle breeze* can be identified today with the many restless desires of our contemporaries, who are seeking wise and patient companions for the journey, their hearts capable of unguarded acceptance, facilitators of grace, not controllers of it, through new seasons of brotherhood and salvation.[87]

Leadership "Behind the People"

12. It is also indispensable that the exodus be made together, conducted with simplicity and clarity by those who serve in authority, with the search for the face of the Lord as the primary goal. Let us invite those who are called to this service to exercise it in obedience to the Spirit, with courage and constancy, so that complexity and transition may be managed, but not slowed or stopped.

Let us encourage leadership that does not leave things the way they are,[88] that banishes the risk that "in the face of the resistance of some members of the community and of certain questions that seem irresoluble, he or she can be tempted to cave in and to consider every effort for

---

87 See Pope Francis, Apostolic Exhortation *Evangelii Gaudium* (November 24, 2013), no. 47.

88 See Pope Francis, Apostolic Exhortation *Evangelii Gaudium* (November 24, 2013), no. 25.

improving the situation useless. What we see here then is the danger of becoming managers of the routine, resigned to mediocrity, restrained from intervening, no longer having the courage to point out the purposes of authentic consecrated life and running the risk of losing the love of one's first fervor and the desire to witness to it."[89]

There is so little time for the small things, for the humility that knows how to offer a few loaves and two fish for God's blessing (see Jn 6:9), and knows how to glimpse in the "'cloud as small as a man's hand'" the coming of the rain (1 Kgs 18:44). We are not called to a preoccupied and administrative leadership, but to a service of authority that, with evangelical clarity, guides the journey to be undertaken together and in unity of heart, within a fragile present in which the future is waiting to be born. We do not need "'mere administration'"[90]; what we need is "to walk after them, helping those who lag behind and—above all—allowing the flock to strike out on new paths."[91]

We need leadership that welcomes and encourages with empathic tenderness the gaze of the brothers and sisters, even of those who force the pace or who impede progress, helping them to overcome haste, fears and attitudes of resistance. Some may hanker to return to the past, some

---

89 Congregation for Institutes of Consecrated Life and Societies of Apostolic Life, Instruction *The Service of Authority and Obedience. Faciem tuam, Domine, Requiram* (May 11, 2008), no. 28.

90 Pope Francis, Apostolic Exhortation *Evangelii Gaudium* (November 24, 2013), no. 25.

91 Ibid., 31.

will nostalgically emphasize the differences, others may brood in silence or raise doubts about the scarcity of means, resources, persons. We should not "cling to a nostalgia for structures and customs which are no longer life-giving in today's world."[92]

We might hear an echo of Elijah's servant who repeats, searching the horizon, "There is nothing." (1 Kgs 18:43). We are called to the grace of patience, to wait and return to searching the sky even seven times, as many times as it takes, so that the journey of us all is not stopped by the indolence of a few:

"To the weak I became weak, to win over the weak. I have become all things to all, to save at least some. All this I do for the sake of the gospel, so that I too may have a share in it" (1 Cor 9:22-23).

May we be given to know how to orient our fraternal journey toward freedom according to the rhythms and seasons of God. Searching the sky together and keeping watch means that we are all of us—individuals, communities, institutes—called to obedience so as "to enter into an order of values which is 'other,' taking on a new and different sense of reality," believing that God has passed by even if he has not left visible footprints, but we have known him only as a voice of sounding silence,[93] and so "experiencing an unthought-of freedom to reach the threshold of the

---

92   Pope Francis, Apostolic Exhortation *Evangelii Gaudium* (November 24, 2013), no. 108.

93   A more literal translation than *soft breeze* for 1 Kgs 19:12.

mystery: 'For my thoughts are not your thoughts, nor are your ways my ways, says the Lord. As high as the heavens are above the earth, so high are my ways above your ways and my thoughts above your thoughts' (Is 55:8-9)."[94]

This exodus intimidates our human logic, which wants clear goals and trodden paths, and a question rings out: who will strengthen our *trembling knees* (see Is 35:3)?

The action of the Spirit in complex and entangled situations manifests itself in the heart as someone who makes things simpler, highlights priorities and offers suggestions for proceeding toward the destinations toward which he wants to take us. It is best, always, to set out in company with the Spirit's breath of joy; "the Spirit itself intercedes with inexpressible groanings. . . . because it intercedes for the holy ones according to God's will" (Rom 8:26-27). "There is no greater freedom than that of allowing oneself to be guided by the Holy Spirit, renouncing the attempt to plan and control everything to the last detail, and instead letting him enlighten, guide and direct us, leading us wherever he wills. The Holy Spirit knows well what is needed in every time and place. This is what it means to be mysteriously fruitful!"[95]

---

94   Congregation for Institutes of Consecrated Life and Societies of Apostolic Life, Instruction *The Service of Authority and Obedience. Faciem tuam, Domine, Requiram* (May 11, 2008), no. 7.

95   Pope Francis, Apostolic Exhortation *Evangelii Gaudium* (November 24, 2013), no. 280.

The Mysticism of the Encounter

13. As "'sentinels' who keep the longing for God alive in the world and reawaken it in the hearts of many people, as well as a thirst for the infinite,"[96] we are called to be seekers of and witnesses to visible and life-giving Gospel plans. We need to be men and women of strong faith, but also with a capacity for empathy, for closeness, and with a spirit both creative and creating; not people who confine the spirit and charism to rigid structures for fear of losing them.

Pope Francis invites us to live the "'mysticism of encounter'": "The ability to hear, to listen to other people. The ability to seek together the way, the method . . . also means not being frightened, not being frightened of things."[97]

The Holy Father continues, "if each of you is a precious opportunity for others to meet with God, it is about rediscovering the responsibility of being prophetic as a community, to seek together, with humility and patience, a word of sense that can be a gift for the country and for the Church, and to bear witness to it with simplicity. You are like *antennas* ready to receive the smallest innovations prompted by the Holy Spirit, and you can help the ecclesial community

---

96   Pope Francis, Address to the Bishops of the Episcopal Conference of Mexico on Their *Ad Limina* Visit, Rome (May 19, 2014).

97   Pope Francis, Address to Rectors and Students of the Pontifical Colleges and Residences of Rome (May 12, 2014).

to take on this gaze of goodness and find new and bold ways to reach all peoples."[98]

One conciliar paradigm was *solicitude for the world and for humanity*. Given that human beings—not in the abstract but in concrete particularity—are "the primary route that the Church must travel in fulfilling her mission,"[99] our efforts on behalf of the men and women of our time remain primary for us. This commitment has always existed, and always been imaginatively renewed: in education, in healthcare, in catechesis, in constant companionship to people with their needs, aspirations, and failings. People in their physical nature, in their social reality: this is the site of evangelization. Consecrated life has gone to the outskirts of the cities, making a true "exodus" to the poor, addressing itself to the world of the abandoned. We must acknowledge exemplary generosity here, but also note that there has been no lack of tensions and risk of lapsing into ideology, above all in the first years after the Council.

"The old story of the Samaritan has been the model of the spirituality of the council. A feeling of boundless sympathy has permeated the whole of it. The attention of our council has been absorbed by the discovery of human needs (and these needs grow in proportion to the greatness which the son of the earth claims for himself). But we call

---

98 Pope Francis, Address to Participants at the General Assembly of the Italian Conference of Secular Institutes, Rome (May 10, 2014).

99 Pope John Paul II, Encyclical Letter *Redemptor Hominis* (March 4, 1979), no. 14.

upon those who term themselves modern humanists, and who have renounced the transcendent value of the highest realities, to give the council credit at least for one quality and to recognize our own new type of humanism: we, too, in fact, we more than any others, honor mankind."[100]

Our mission presents itself in terms of this "sympathy," in terms of the centrality of the person who knows how to begin with the human. Bringing out all the richness and truth of humanity that the encounter with Christ demands and fosters introduces us, at the same time, to the understanding that ecclesial resources are important precisely as resources of true humanity and *human promotion*.[101] But what sort of men and women do we have before us? What are the challenges to, and innovations necessary for, a consecrated life that means to live according to the "style" of the Council, meaning in an attitude of dialogue and solidarity, of profound and authentic "sympathy" with the men and women of today and their culture, their deepest "feelings," their self-awareness, their moral coordinates?

Moved by the Spirit of Christ, we are called to recognize what is truly human. Otherwise our actions would (as Pope Francis has repeatedly said)[102] take on the social character of a pious NGO, aiming to build a more just society, but one

---

100 Pope Paul VI, Address During the Last General Meeting of the Second Vatican Council, Rome (December 7, 1965).

101 See Sacred Congregation for Religious and Secular Institutes, *Religious [Persons] and Human Promotion*, Rome (August 12, 1980).

102 See Pope Francis, Homily at Holy Mass with the Cardinal Electors, Rome (March 14, 2013).

that is secularized, closed to transcendence, and ultimately is not just either. Goals of social development must occur in a landscape that presents and protects the witness of the Kingdom and the truth of the human being.

In our time, which is dominated by pervasive and global communication, and at the same time by an inability to communicate with authenticity, consecrated life is called to be a sign of the possibility of human relationships that are welcoming, transparent and sincere. Faced with humanity's weakness and its alienating and self-referential solitude, the Church is counting on communities of brothers and sisters rich "'with joy and with the Holy Spirit' (Acts 13:52)."[103] Consecrated life, a particular school of love (*specialis caritatis schola*),[104] is shaped in its manifold forms of fraternity by the Holy Spirit, because "where the community is, there is the Spirit of God; and where the Spirit of God is, there is the community and all grace."[105]

We esteem community as a place rich in mystery and "*a special experience of the light which shines forth from the Incarnate Word.*"[106] One can perceive a gap between this mystery and daily life: we are called to move from a mere form of life in common to the grace of fraternity; from the

---

103 See Pope John Paul II, Post-Synodal Apostolic Exhortation, *Vita Consecrata* (March 25, 1996), no. 45.

104 William of St. Thierry, *De Natura et Dignitate Amoris*, 9, 26.

105 Irenaeus of Lyon, *Against Heresies*, III, 24, I.

106 Pope John Paul II, Post-Synodal Apostolic Exhortation *Vita Consecrata* (March 25, 1996), no. 42; see Second Vatican Council, *Decree on the Adaptation and Renewal of Religious Life (Perfectae Caritatis)*, no. 15.

forma communis to human relations after the pattern of the Gospel, by virtue of the love of God poured out into our hearts by means of the Holy Spirit (see Rom 5:5).

Pope Francis cautions us: "It always pains me greatly to discover how some Christian communities, and even consecrated persons, can tolerate different forms of enmity, division, calumny, defamation, vendetta, jealousy and the desire to impose certain ideas at all costs, even to persecutions which appear as veritable witch hunts. Whom are we going to evangelize if this is the way we act? . . . No one is saved by himself or herself, individually, or by his or her own efforts. God attracts us by taking into account the complex interweaving of personal relationships entailed in the life of a human community."[107]

We are called, then, to see ourselves as a fraternity open to the complementarity of meeting in fellowship those who are different, so as to grow in unity: "Nor do people who wholeheartedly enter into the life of a community need to lose their individualism or hide their identity; instead, they receive new impulses to personal growth."[108] The style of "dialogue" that "is much more than the communication of a truth. It arises from the enjoyment of speaking and it enriches those who express their love for one another through the medium of words. This is an enrichment which does not consist in objects but in persons who share

---

107 Pope Francis, Apostolic Exhortation *Evangelii Gaudium* (November 24, 2013), nos. 100, 113.

108 Ibid., no. 235; see no. 131.

themselves in dialogue."[109] We remember that "dialogue thrives on friendship, and most especially on service."[110]

May our communities be places where the mystery of the human touches the divine mystery, in the experience of the Gospel. There are two privileged "sites" in which the Gospel manifests itself, takes shape, and gives itself: the family and consecrated life. In the first of these, the family, the Gospel enters into the everyday and shows its capacity to transfigure the manner in which we live this, in a landscape of love. The second sign, an image of the future world that puts every good of this world into perspective, becomes a place that mirrors the first and complements it, while it demonstrates in advance the fulfilment of life's journey and places even the most rewarding of all human experiences in relationship to the final communion with God.[111]

We become a "site of the Gospel" when we secure for ourselves and for the benefit of all a place of attentiveness to God, to prevent time from being filled entirely with things, activities and words. We are sites of the Gospel when we are women and men who desire: who await an encounter, a reunion, a relationship. This is why it is essential that our rhythms of life, community settings and all

---

109 Ibid., no. 142.

110 Pope Paul VI, Encyclical Letter *Ecclesiam Suam* (August 6, 1964), no. 87; see Pope Francis, Address to Participants at the General Assembly of the Italian Conference of Secular Institutes, Rome (May 10, 2014).

111 See Thirteenth Ordinary General Assembly of the Synod of Bishops, Message to the People of God, October 7-28, 2012, no. 7.

our activities become places that preserve an "absence": an absence which is the presence of God.

"The community supports the whole of the apostolate. At times religious communities are fraught with *tensions*, and risk becoming individualistic and scattered, whereas what is needed is deep communication and authentic relationships. The humanizing power of the Gospel is witnessed in *fraternity lived* in community and is created through welcome, respect, mutual help, understanding, kindness, forgiveness and joy."[112]

The community in this way becomes a home in which we live according to the difference made by the Gospel. The style of the Gospel, human and sober, is shown in the search that aspires to transfiguration; in celibacy for the sake of the Kingdom; in the search for and listening to God and his Word: in obedience that demonstrates the Christian difference. These are eloquent signs in a world that is turning back to seek what is essential.

The community that sits at table and recognizes Jesus in the breaking of the bread (see Lk 24:13-35) is also the place in which each one recognizes his frailty. Fraternity does not produce perfect relationships, but welcomes the limitations of all and takes them to heart and to prayer as a wound inflicted on the commandment of love (see Jn 13:31-35): a place where the Paschal mystery brings healing and where unity grows. This is an event of grace invoked and received

---

112 Pope Francis, Address to Participants in the General Chapter of the Salesian Society of St. John Bosco (Salesians), Rome (March 31, 2014).

by brothers and sisters who are together not by choice but by calling; it is an experience of the presence of the Risen One.

The Prophecy That Mediates

14. Religious families are born to inspire new journeys, suggest unforeseen routes, or respond nimbly to human needs and necessities of the spirit. Sometimes, an institution can become loaded over time with "obsolete laws,"[113] and society's needs may turn Gospel answers into responses calibrated for "business" efficiency and rationality. It can happen that consecrated life loses its authoritativeness, the boldness of its charism and its evangelical truth-telling (*parrhesia*), lured on by lights extraneous to its identity.

Pope Francis calls us to creative fidelity; to God's surprises: "Jesus can also break through the dull categories with which we would enclose him and he constantly amazes us by his divine creativity. Whenever we make the effort to return to the source and to recover the original freshness of the Gospel, new avenues arise, new paths of creativity open up, with different forms of expression, more eloquent signs

---

113 Second Vatican Council, *Decree on the Adaptation and Renewal of Religious Life (Perfectae Caritatis)*, no. 3.

and words with new meaning for today's world. Every form of authentic evangelization is always 'new'."[114]

At the Crossroads of the World

15. The Spirit calls us to modulate the *servitium caritatis* according to the insight of the Church. Charity "demands justice: recognition and respect for the legitimate rights of individuals and peoples. It strives to build the *earthly city* according to law and justice. On the other hand, charity transcends justice and completes it in the logic of giving and forgiving. The *earthly city* is promoted not merely by relationships of rights and duties, but to an even greater and more fundamental extent by relationships of gratuitousness, mercy and communion,"[115] and the Magisterium introduces us to a broader understanding: "The risk for our time is that the *de facto* interdependence of people and nations is not matched by ethical interaction of consciences and minds that would give rise to truly human development. Only in *charity, illumined by the light of reason and faith*, is it possible to pursue development goals that possess a more humane and humanizing value."[116]

Other promptings of the Spirit call us to strengthen citadels in which thought and study may protect human

---

114 Pope Francis, Apostolic Exhortation *Evangelii Gaudium* (November 24, 2013), no. 11.

115 Pope Benedict XVI, Encyclical Letter *Caritas in Veritate* (June 29, 2009), no. 6.

116 Ibid., no. 9.

identity and its aspect of grace, amidst the flow of digital connections and the world of networks, which express a real (and spiritual) condition of contemporary man. Technology nurtures and at the same time communicates needs, and stimulates desires that human beings have always had: we are called to inhabit these *unexplored lands* in order to tell them about the Gospel. "Today, when the networks and means of human communication have made unprecedented advances, we sense the challenge of finding and sharing a 'mystique' of living together, of mingling and encounter, of embracing and supporting one another, of stepping into this flood tide which, while chaotic, can become a genuine experience of fraternity, a caravan of solidarity, a sacred pilgrimage."[117]

We are similarly called to pitch our tents at the crossroads of untrodden paths. We are called to stand at the threshold, like the prophet Elijah, who made the geography of the periphery a resource of revelation: to the north at Zarephath, to the south at Horeb, to the east beyond the Jordan into penitent solitude and, finally, to the ascension into heaven. The *threshold* is the place where the Spirit groans aloud: there where we no longer know what to say, nor what to expect, but where the Spirit knows the *plans of God* (see Rom 8:27) and hands them over to us. There is the risk, at times, of attributing our long-established maps to the ways of the Spirit, because we find it reassuring always

---

117 Pope Francis, Apostolic Exhortation *Evangelii Gaudium* (November 24, 2013), no. 87.

to travel by the same roads. Pope Benedict declared himself open to the vision of a Church that grows *by attraction*,[118] while Pope Francis dreams of "a missionary impulse capable of transforming everything, so that the Church's customs, ways of doing things, times and schedules, language and structures can be suitably channeled for the evangelization of today's world rather than for her self-preservation . . . a constant desire to go forth and in this way to elicit a positive response from all those whom Jesus summons to friendship with himself."[119]

The joy of the Gospel calls us to weave a spirituality like a type of searching, exploring alternative metaphors and new images, and creating unprecedented perspectives. Humbly starting anew from the experience of Christ and his Gospel, it finds a wisdom that is experiential and often unarmed, like David before Goliath. The power of the Gospel, which we experience as salvation and joy, enables us wisely to use images and symbols suitable for a culture that soaks up events, thoughts, and values, and continually recasts them as seductive "icons," an echo of "a deep longing for God in many peoples' hearts, which is expressed in

---

118 Pope Benedict XVI, Homily at the Holy Mass for the Inauguration of the Fifth General Conference of the Bishops of Latin America and the Caribbean at the Shrine of Aparecida, Aparecida, Brazil (May 13, 2007).

119 Pope Francis, Apostolic Exhortation *Evangelii Gaudium* (November 24, 2013), no. 27.

different ways and impels numerous men and women to set out on a path of sincere seeking."[120]

In the past one of the most vigorous themes of spiritual life was the symbol of the *voyage* or the *ascent*: not in space, but toward the center of the soul. This mystical process, laid as the foundation of the life of the spirit, today encounters other valuable ideas shedding light and offering meaning. These include prayer, purification, the exercise of virtues relating to social solidarity, inculturation, spiritual ecumenism, a new anthropology, the call for a new hermeneutic and, following ancient patristic tradition, new paths of mystagogy.

Consecrated men and women, familiar with the Spirit and well aware of the inner man in whom Christ dwells, are called to move along these paths, opposing the *dia-bolical* that divides and separates, and liberating the *sym-bolical*, meaning the primacy of the bond and relationship present in the complexity of created reality, "as a plan for the fullness of times, to sum up all things in Christ, in heaven and on earth" (Eph 1:10).

Where will the consecrated be? The evangelical form of life they profess has freed them from their shackles; will they be able to stay, like watchmen, at the edge of things, where the gaze becomes more clear, more penetrating, and thought more humble? Will consecrated life as a whole be

120 Pope Benedict XVI, Letter to Cardinal Kurt Koch, President of the Pontifical Council for Christian Unity, on the Occasion of the Twelveth Inter-Christian Symposium (Thessaloniki, August 29–September 2, 2011).

able to welcome the challenge of questions that come from the crossroads of the world?

The experience of the poor, interreligious and intercultural dialogue, the complementarity of man and woman, environmentalism in a sick world, eugenics without scruples, a globalized economy, planetary communication, symbolic language: these are the new hermeneutical horizons that cannot simply be enumerated, but must be inhabited and brought firmly under the guidance of the Spirit who groans aloud in all of them (see Rom 8:22-27). These are epoch-making avenues of exploration that call into question values, languages, priorities, anthropologies. Millions of people are on a journey through worlds and civilizations, destabilizing age-old identities and fostering mixtures of cultures and religions.

Can consecrated life become a welcoming dialogue partner "in the search for God which has always stirred the human heart"?[121] Will it be able to go, like Paul, into the public square of Athens and speak of the unknown God to the *gentiles* (see Acts 17:22-34)? Will it be able to foster the ardor of thought needed to recognize anew the value of otherness and the ethical question of how difference may peacefully coexist?

Consecrated life, in its diverse forms, is already present at these crossroads. For centuries, beginning with the monasteries, communities and fraternities in border territories

---

121 Pope John Paul II, Post-Synodal Apostolic Exhortation *Vita Consecrata* (March 25, 1996), no. 103.

have lived out their silent witness as sites of the Gospel, of dialogue, of encounter. Many consecrated men and women also live in the everyday world of today's men and women, sharing their joys and sorrows in the bustling pattern of time, with the wisdom and boldness to "find new and bold ways to reach all" in Christ,[122] and "going beyond, not only beyond, but beyond and in between . . . where everything is at stake."[123]

Consecrated men and women on the threshold (*limen*) are called to open "clearings," as was done in the distant past when spaces were opened in the woods for the founding of cities. As Pope Francis emphasizes, the consequences of such choices are uncertain; they undoubtedly require us to leave the center and travel toward the peripheries, and demand a redistribution of forces in which what predominates is not safeguarding the *status quo* and the bottom line, but the prophetic witness of Gospel choices. "The charism is not a bottle of distilled water. It must be lived energetically, reinterpreting it culturally as well."[124]

Under the Banner of the Least

16. Let us continue our voyage of putting meditations together under the humble banner of the Gospel: "Never

---

122 See Pope Francis, Address to Participants in the General Assembly of the Italian Conference of Secular Institutes, Rome (May 10, 2014).

123 Ibid.

124 A. Spadaro, "Svegliate il Mondo!" Conversation of Pope Francis with Superiors General, in *La Civiltà Cattolica*, 165 (2014/I), 8.

lose the impulse of walking down the roads of the world, the awareness that walking, even going with an uncertain or halting stride is still better than standing still, closed off in our own questions or certainties."[125]

The icons that we have meditated upon—from the cloud that accompanied the exodus to the events of the prophet Elijah—show us that the Kingdom of God is manifested among us under the banner of this least. "Let us believe the Gospel when it tells us that the kingdom of God is already present in this world and is growing, here and there, and in different ways: like the small seed which grows into a great tree (see Mt 13:31-32), like the measure of leaven that makes the dough rise (see Mt 13:33) and like the good seed that grows amid the weeds (see Mt 13:24-30) and can always pleasantly surprise us."[126]

Those who stop at self-referentiality often have an image and awareness only of themselves and of their own horizons. Those who push themselves to the margins may glimpse and foster a more humble and spiritual world.

New pathways of faith are springing up today in humble places, under the banner of a Word that, if listened to and lived, will lead to redemption. The institutes of consecrated life and the societies of apostolic life that make decisions on the basis of little signs interpreted in faith, and in a prophetic role that knows how to intuit what is *beyond*, become

---

125 Ibid.
126 Pope Francis, Apostolic Exhortation *Evangelii Gaudium* (November 24, 2013), no. 278.

places of life where the light shines and the invitation rings out calling others to follow Christ.

Let's plant a small and humble type of work and presence, like the mustard seed in the Gospel (see Mt 13:31-32), where the intensity of the sign should shine without any limits: the courageous word, joyful fraternity, listening to the small voice, the memory of the dwelling-place of God among men. We must cultivate "a contemplative gaze, a gaze of faith which sees God dwelling in their homes, in their streets and squares. God's presence accompanies the sincere efforts of individuals and groups to find encouragement and meaning in their lives. He dwells among them, fostering solidarity, fraternity, and the desire for goodness, truth and justice. This presence must not be contrived but found, uncovered."[127]

Consecrated life finds its fruitfulness not only in bearing witness to the good, but in recognizing it and being able to point it out, especially where it is not usually seen, amongst "'non-citizens,'" "'half-citizens,'" "'urban remnants,'"[128] those without dignity. We must move from words of solidarity to actions that welcome and heal: consecrated life is called to this truth.[129]

---

127 Pope Francis, Apostolic Exhortation *Evangelii Gaudium* (November 24, 2013), no. 71.

128 Ibid., no. 74.

129 See ibid., no. 207.

Pope Benedict urged us:

I invite you to have a faith that can recognize the wisdom of weakness. In the joys and afflictions of the present time, when the harshness and weight of the cross make themselves felt, do not doubt that the *kenosis* of Christ is already a paschal victory. Precisely in our limitations and weaknesses as human beings we are called to live conformation with Christ in an all-encompassing commitment which anticipates the eschatological perfection, to the extent that this is possible in time. In a society of efficiency and success, your life, marked by the "humility" and frailty of the lowly, of empathy with those who have no voice, becomes an evangelical sign of contradiction.[130]

Our invitation is to return to the wisdom of the Gospel, as it is lived by the least (see Mt 11:25): "the joy which we experience daily, amid the little things of life, as a response to the loving invitation of God our Father: 'My child, treat yourself well, according to your means . . . Do not deprive yourself of the day's enjoyment' (Sir 14:11, 14). What tender paternal love echoes in these words!"[131]

---

130 Pope Benedict XVI, Homily for the Feast of the Presentation of the Lord on the Seventeenth World Day of Consecrated Life, Rome (February 2, 2013).

131 Pope Francis, Apostolic Exhortation *Evangelii Gaudium* (November 24, 2013), no. 4.

The current weakness of consecrated life also stems from having lost the joy in "the little things of life."[132] On the way of conversion, consecrated men and women should discover that the primary vocation—as we recalled in the letter *Rejoice!*—is the vocation to joy in welcoming the least and seeking the good: "Just for today I will be happy in the certainty that I have been created for happiness, not only in the next world, but also in this."[133]

Pope Francis calls us to allow ourselves to be "guided by the Holy Spirit, renouncing the attempt to plan and control everything to the last detail, and instead letting him enlighten, guide and direct us, leading us wherever he wills. The Holy Spirit knows well what is needed in every time and place."[134]

In Choir, in the Orans Posture

17. The horizon is open; we are called to prayerful watchfulness, interceding for the world. On the horizon, we continue to see little signs heralding an abundant, beneficial rainfall on our dryness, faint whispers of a faithful presence.

The journey we must make to follow the cloud is not always easy; discernment sometimes demands long and tiring periods of waiting; the light and easy yoke (see Mt 11:30)

---

132   Ibid.

133   Pope John XXIII. Decalogue of Serenity, in *Journal of a Soul* (LEV ed., p. 207)

134   Pope Francis, Apostolic Exhortation *Evangelii Gaudium* (November 24, 2013), no. 280.

can become heavy. The desert is also a place of solitude, of emptiness. It is a place where the fundamentals of life are lacking: water, vegetation, the companionship of others, the warmth of a friend, even life itself. In the desert in silence and in solitude, each of us touches his truest image: he measures himself against the infinite, his own frailty, like a grain of sand, and his rock-like solidity as mystery of God.

The Israelites remained encamped as long as the cloud rested over the tent; they continued their journey when the cloud lifted from that dwelling-place. Stopping and departing again: a life that is guided, regulated, patterned by the cloud of the Spirit; a life to be lived in vigilant watching.

Elijah, curled up in a ball, crushed by pain and by the infidelity of the people, bears his suffering and betrayal on his back and in his heart. He himself becomes prayer, a prayerful beseeching, a womb that intercedes. Beside him, and on his behalf, a boy searches the sky, to see if in answer to God's promise a sign is appearing from the sea.

This is the pattern of the spiritual journey of each one of us, through which man truly becomes a friend of God, an instrument of his divine plan of salvation, becomes aware of his vocation and mission on behalf of all the weak of the earth.

Consecrated life in the present time is called to live with particular intensity the posture (*statio*) of intercession. Let us be aware of our limitations and our finiteness, while our spirit is passing through desert and consolation, through darkness and light, in search of God and the signs of his grace. In this prayerful posture what is at stake is the rebellious obedience of the prophetic function of conse-crated life, which makes itself a passionate voice on behalf of humanity. Fullness and emptiness—as a profound per-ception of the mystery of God, the world, and the human—are experiences we go through with equal intensity on the journey.

Pope Francis has a direct question for us: "Do you strug-gle with the Lord for your people, as Abraham struggled? Suppose they were fewer? Suppose there were twenty-five? And suppose they were twenty? (see Gen 18:22-33). This courageous prayer of intercession. . . . We speak of *parrhesia*, of apostolic courage, and we think of pastoral plans, this is good, but the same *parrhesia* is also needed in prayer."[135]

Intercession makes itself the voice of human poverty, arrival and outcome (*adventus et eventus*): preparation for the response of grace, the fertility of arid soil, the mysticism of encounter under the of little things.

The capacity to sit praying in choir makes consecrated men and women not solitary prophets, but men and women of communion, of a shared listening to the Word, capable of elaborating together new signs and significances, con-ceived and constructed even during times of persecution and martyrdom. This is a journey toward the communion of differences: a sign of the Spirit who breathes passion into hearts so that all may be one (Jn 17:22). In this way is revealed a Church that, sitting at table after a journey

---

135   Pope Francis, Address to the Parish Priests of the Diocese of Rome, March 6, 2014.

of doubts and sad, hopeless talk, recognizes the Lord in the breaking of bread (Lk 24:13-35), clothed anew in the essence of the Gospel.

FOR REFLECTION

18. The Paradoxes of Pope Francis

- "When the Lord wants to give us a mission, he wants to give us a task, he prepares us to do it well," just "like he prepared Elijah." The important thing is "not that you've encountered the Lord" but "the whole journey to accomplish the mission that the Lord entrusted to you." And this is precisely "the difference between the apostolic mission that the Lord gives us and a good, honest, human task." Thus "when the Lord bestows a mission, he always employs a process of purification, a process of perception, a process of obedience, a process of prayer."[136]

- "Are they meek and humble? In the community, is there quarrelling among them over power, are there battles due to envy? Is there gossiping? If so, then they are not on the path of Jesus Christ." Indeed, . . . peace in a community is "such an important feature." "It is so important because the devil seeks to divide us, always. He is the father of division; through envy he divides.

---

136 Pope Francis, Morning Meditation in the Chapel of the *Domus Sanctae Marthae*, Rome (June 13, 2014).

Jesus enables us to see this path, that of peace among us, of love among us."[137]

- In this regard . . . it is important, "to be in the habit of asking for the grace to remember the journey which the People of God made." It is also important to ask for the grace of "personal memory: what has God done with me in my life? How has he had me journey?" We also need to know how "to ask for the grace of hope, which is not optimism: it is something else." Finally, . . . let us "ask for the grace to renew each day our covenant with the Lord who has called us." May the Lord, he prayed, "grant us these three graces which are necessary for one's Christian identity.'"[138]

- This . . . "is our destiny: to walk with a view to the promises, confident that they will become a reality. It is beautiful to read Chapter 11 of the Letter to the Hebrews, where the journey of the People of God toward the promises is recounted. This people so loved the promises, they sought them even to the point of martyrdom. They knew that God was faithful. Hope never disappoints." . . . "This is our life: to believe and

---

137 Pope Francis, Morning Meditation in the Chapel of the *Domus Sanctae Marthae*, Rome (April 29, 2014).

138 Pope Francis, Morning Meditation in the Chapel of the *Domus Sanctae Marthae*, Rome (May 15, 2014).

take to the road" like Abram, who "trusted in the Lord and also journeyed amid hardship and difficulty."[139]

- Never lose the momentum of *walking the streets* of the world, aware that walking, even with an uncertain step or limping along, is always better than standing still, withdrawn in your own questions or sense of security. The missionary passion, the joy of the encounter with Christ that urges you to share with others the beauty of faith, reduces the risk of becoming stuck in individualism.[140]

- Religious men and women are prophets. They are those who have chosen a following of Jesus that imitates his life in obedience to the Father, poverty, community life and chastity. In this sense, the vows cannot end up being caricatures; otherwise, for example, community life becomes hell, and chastity becomes a way of life for unfruitful bachelors. The vow of chastity must be a vow of fruitfulness. In the church, the religious are called to be prophets in particular by demonstrating how Jesus lived on this earth, and to proclaim how the kingdom

---

139 Pope Francis, Morning Meditation in the Chapel of the *Domus Sanctae Marthae*, Rome (March 31, 2014).

140 Pope Francis, Address to Participants in the General Assembly of the Italian Conference of Secular Institutes, Rome (May 10, 2014).

of God will be in its perfection. A religious must never give up prophecy.[141]

- Vigilance: this is a Christian attitude. Vigilance over one's self: what is happening in my heart? Because where my heart is, there my treasure will be. What is happening there? The Eastern Fathers say that I must know well if my heart is in turmoil or if my heart is calm. . . . Then, what do I do? I try to understand what is happening, but always in peace—to understand in peace. Then peace returns and I can perform the *discussio conscientiae*. When I am in peace and there is no turmoil: "What happened today in my heart?" And this is *keeping watch*. Keeping watch is not a matter of entering a torture chamber, no! It is watching one's heart. We must be *masters* over our heart. What does my heart feel, what does it seek? What made me happy today, and what didn't make me happy?[142]

- Thanks be to God, you do not live or work as isolated individuals but as a community: and thank God for this! The community supports the whole of the apostolate. At times religious communities are fraught with *tensions*, and risk becoming individualistic and

---

141 A. Spadaro, Interview with Pope Francis, in *La Civiltà Cattolica* III (2013). English translation published as "A Big Heart Open to God," *America Magazine*, September 30, 2013.

142 Pope Francis, Address to Rectors and Students of Pontifical Colleges and Residences of Rome, Rome (May 12, 2014).

scattered, whereas what is needed is deep communication and authentic relationships. The humanizing power of the Gospel is witnessed in *fraternity lived* in community and is created through welcome, respect, mutual help, understanding, kindness, forgiveness and joy.[143]

- You are a leaven that can produce good bread for many, the Bread for which there is so much hunger: listening to people's needs, aspirations, disappointments, hopes. Like those who have preceded you in your vocation, you can restore hope to young people, help the elderly, open roads to the future, spread love in every place and in every situation. If this does not happen, if your ordinary life lacks witness and prophecy, then, I repeat to you, there is an urgent need for conversion![144]

- Instead of being just a church that welcomes and receives by keeping the doors open, let us try also to be a church that finds new roads, that is able to step outside itself and go to those who do not attend Mass, to those who have left or are indifferent. The ones who leave sometimes do it for reasons that, if properly

---

143 Pope Francis, Address to Participants in the General Chapter of the Salesian Society of St. John Bosco (Salesians), Rome (March 31, 2014).

144 Pope Francis, Address to Participants in the General Assembly of the Italian Conference of Secular Institutes, Rome (May 10, 2014).

understood and assessed, can lead to a return. But that takes audacity and courage.[145]

• And in the consecrated life we live the encounter between the young and the old, between observation and prophecy. Let's not see these as two opposing realities! Let us rather allow the Holy Spirit to animate both of them, and a sign of this is joy: the joy of observing, of walking within a rule of life; the joy of being led by the Spirit, never unyielding, never closed, always open to the voice of God that speaks, that opens, that leads us and invites us to go toward the horizon.[146]

Hail, Woman of the New Covenant

19. To walk following the signs of God means experiencing the joy and renewed enthusiasm of the encounter with Christ,[147] center of life and source of decisions and actions.[148]

---

145 A. Spadaro, Interview with Pope Francis, in *La Civiltà Cattolica* III (2013). English translation published as "A Big Heart Open to God," *America Magazine*, September 30, 2013.

146 Pope Francis, Homily for the Feast of the Presentation of the Lord on the Eighteenth World Day of Consecrated Life, Rome (February 2, 2014).

147 See Pope Benedict XVI, Apostolic Letter in the form *motu proprio, Porta Fidei*, with which he proclaimed the Year of Faith (October 11, 2011), no. 2.

148 Congregation for institutes of Consecrated Life and Societies of Apostolic Life, Instruction *Starting Afresh from Christ: A Renewed Commitment to Consecrated Life in the Third Millennium* (May 19, 2002).

The encounter with the Lord is renewed day after day in the joy of a persevering journey. "Always on the road borne along by the virtue that is of pilgrims: joy!"[149]

Our days call for the necessity of vigilance:

> Keeping watch . . . It is watching one's heart. We must be *masters* over our heart. What does my heart feel, what does it seek? What made me happy today, and what didn't make me happy? . . . This is for the purpose of knowing the state of my heart, my life, how I am walking on the path of the Lord. For if there is no vigilance, the heart goes everywhere, and the imagination follows behind: "go, go . . ." and then one might not end up well. I like the question about vigilance. These are not ancient things of times past, we haven't gone beyond these things.[150]

The consecrated person becomes *memoria Dei*: he or she recalls the action of the Lord. The time given us to follow the cloud requires perseverance, faithfulness in keeping watch "as if seeing the one who is invisible" (Heb 11:27). It is the time of the new covenant. In fragmented days with only short breathing-spaces, we are asked, like Elijah, to keep watch, to search the horizon without weariness looking

---

149 Pope Francis, Address to Participants in the Genneral Assembly of the Italian Conference of Secular Institutes, Rome (May 10, 2014).

150 Pope Francis, Address to Rectors and Students of Pontifical Colleges and Residences of Rome, Rome (May 12, 2014).

for the "'cloud as small as a man's hand'" (1 Kgs 18:44); we are asked to keep up bold perseverance and a clear vision of eternity. Our time remains a time of exile, of pilgrimage, of watchful and joyful expectation of the eschatological reality in which God will be all in all.

Mary "was the new Ark of the Covenant, before which the heart exults with joy, the Mother of God present in the world who does not keep this divine presence to herself but offers it, sharing the grace of God. Thus, the prayer says, Mary really is the *causa nostrae laetitae*, the 'Ark' in whom the Savior is truly present among us."[151]

Hail Mary, Woman of the New Covenant, we call you blessed because you have believed (see Lk 1:45) and have known how "to recognize the traces of God's Spirit in events great and small."[152]

You sustain our watching in the night, until the light of dawn anticipates the new day. Grant us a prophet's voice to tell the world about the joy of the Gospel, about the blessedness of those who search the horizons of new lands and heavens (see Rev 21:1) and anticipate their presence in the human city.

Help us to proclaim the fecundity of the Spirit under the banner of the essential and the small. Grant that we may perform, here and now, the courageous act

---

151 Pope Benedict XVI, Homily for the Solemnity of the Assumption of the Blessed Virgin Mary, Castel Gandolfo (August 15, 2011).

152 Pope Francis, Apostolic Exhortation *Evangelii Gaudium* (November 24, 2013), no. 288.

of the humble, upon whom God looks (see Ps 138:6) and to whom are revealed the secrets of the Kingdom (see Mt 11:25-26).

Amen.

> From the Vatican, September 8, 2014
> Nativity of the Blessed Virgin Mary
> Cardinal João Braz de Aviz
> Prefect

> ✠ José Rodríguez Carballo, OFM
> Archbishop's Secretary